WORLD BOOK

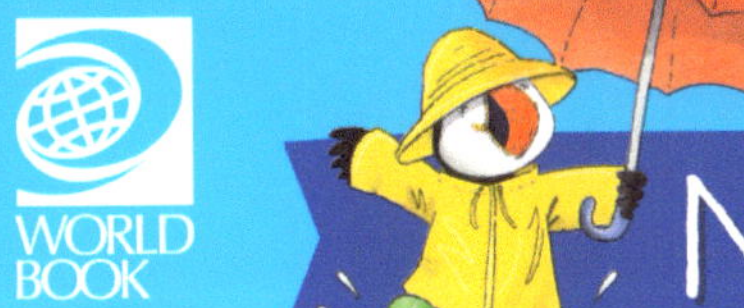

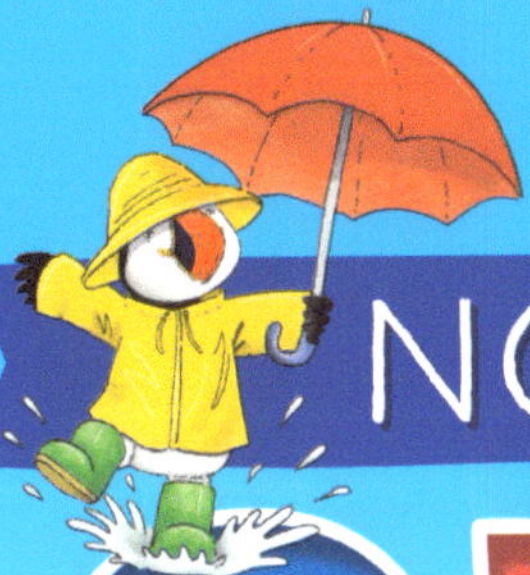

NORRIE EXPLORES... LONDON

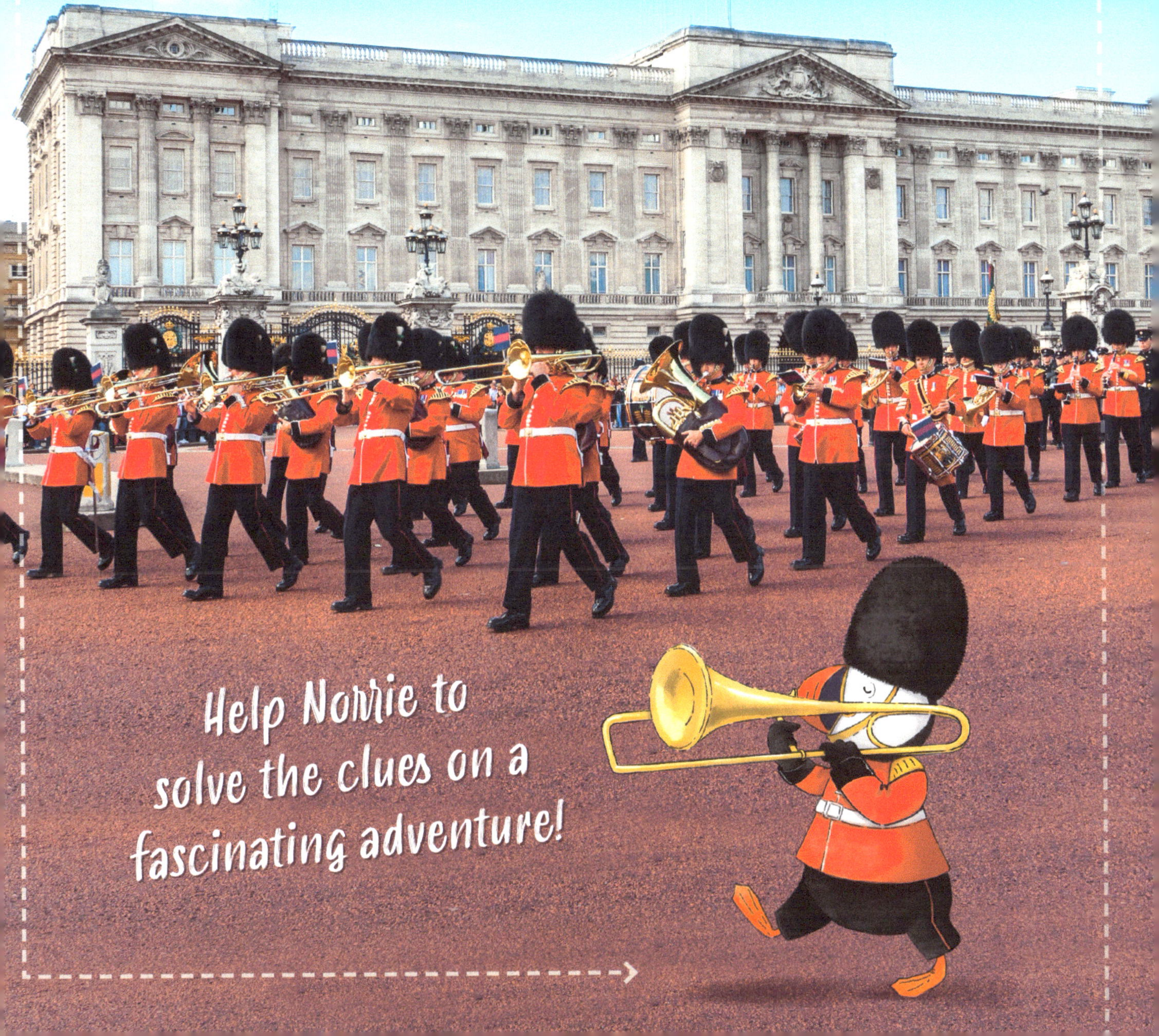

Help Norrie to solve the clues on a fascinating adventure!

World Book, Inc.
180 North LaSalle Street
Suite 900
Chicago, Illinois 60601
USA

For information about other World Book publications, visit our website at www.worldbook.com or call 1-800-WORLDBK (967-5325). For information about sales to schools and libraries, call 1-800-975-3250 (United States), or 1-800-837-5365 (Canada).

Library of Congress Cataloging-in-Publication Data for this volume has been applied for.

Norrie Explores ...
ISBN: 978-0-7166-5303-5 (set, hc.)

Norrie Explores ... London
ISBN: 978-0-7166-5308-0 (hc.)
ISBN: 978-0-7166-5328-8 (pf.)

Also available as:
ISBN: 978-0-7166-5318-9 (e-book)

Staff

Acknowledgments

Writer: Izzi Howell
Illustrator: Lizzie Walkley

Developed with World Book by
White-Thomson Publishing LTD
www.wtpub.co.uk

Cover: Norrie artwork by Lizzie Walkley, Advocate Art; © Alex Segre, Shutterstock

3 © Album/Alamy Images
4-9 © Shutterstock
10-11 © cowardlion/Shutterstock; © Jon Arnold Images Ltd/Alamy Images
12-13 © Luke MacGregor, Reuters/Alamy Images; © cowardlion/Shutterstock; © skovalsky/Shutterstock
14-15 © John Kellerman, Alamy Images; © fotoVoyager/iStock; © Sergii Figurnyi, Shutterstock
16-17 © Nathaniel Noir, Alamy Images; © Angelina Dimitrova, Shutterstock
18-19 © Zoonar GmbH/Alamy Images; © azmanq/Shutterstock
20-21 © David Herraez Calzada, Shutterstock; © Album/Alamy Images; © Bokeh Blur Background/Shutterstock
22-23 © Shutterstock
24-25 © Sam Barnes, Alamy Images; © pcruciatti/Shutterstock; © Toby Melville, Reuters/Alamy Images
26-27 © Shutterstock
28-29 © William Barton, Alamy Images; © John Michaels, Alamy Images; © Angelo Hornak, Alamy Images; © Alex Segre, Shutterstock
30-35 © Shutterstock
36-37 © Tim M, Shutterstock; © Mo Peerbacus, Alamy Images; © Alex Segre, Alamy Images
38-39 © Kiev.Victor, Shutterstock; © ZGPhotography/Shutterstock; Transport for London; © neelsky/Shutterstock
40-51 © Shutterstock

Contents

Help me solve the clues on my journey through London!

Whew! It's quite an adventure!

Welcome to London!

Hi, I'm Norrie! I'm a puffin. I love to travel the world and explore different cities around the globe.

Today, I'm in London, England, which is a part of the United Kingdom. The United Kingdom is a nation in Europe. London is the capital city of the United Kingdom. Have you ever visited London before?

London is one of the oldest and most important cities in the world. It was founded by the Romans nearly 2,000 years ago. They called it Londinium *(luhn DIHN ee uhm)*. Today, London is home to over 9 million people!

London is packed full of interesting places and amazing buildings. I can't wait to see them for myself! It's going to be a great trip.

As well as traveling, I also love puzzles! My friend Lord Percival Pigeon, who lives in London, has challenged me to a London treasure hunt. Just like my favorite British detective, Sherlock Holmes, I need to solve clues and riddles. The clues will be photos, words, or objects that will give me a hint about the next place to visit. Following the clues will help me find my way around the city and see some of the best places to visit in London! Off we go!

Tower of London

I feel just like Sherlock Holmes! I've solved my first clue and found my first place to visit – the Tower of London! This building is a very old castle. Over the years, it has been used as a palace, a prison, and a place to keep treasure. Its oldest section is the White Tower in the center. It was built by a king called William the Conqueror between 1078 and 1097. The tower is still used to store treasure. The Crown Jewels are kept inside. These are crowns and scepters (which are a sort of fancy rod) used by kings and queens. Some of the Crown Jewels are still worn by members of the royal family on special occasions!

A beefeater giving a tour of the Tower of London.
The Tower of London is guarded by big black birds called ravens. Seven ravens live here at the tower. Six are on guard while one is extra. An old legend says that England will end if the ravens leave the tower grounds! The ravens' wing feathers are clipped so they can't fly away.
Nice to make a local friend!
One down ... I'm ready for my next clue!
Don't forget the fire

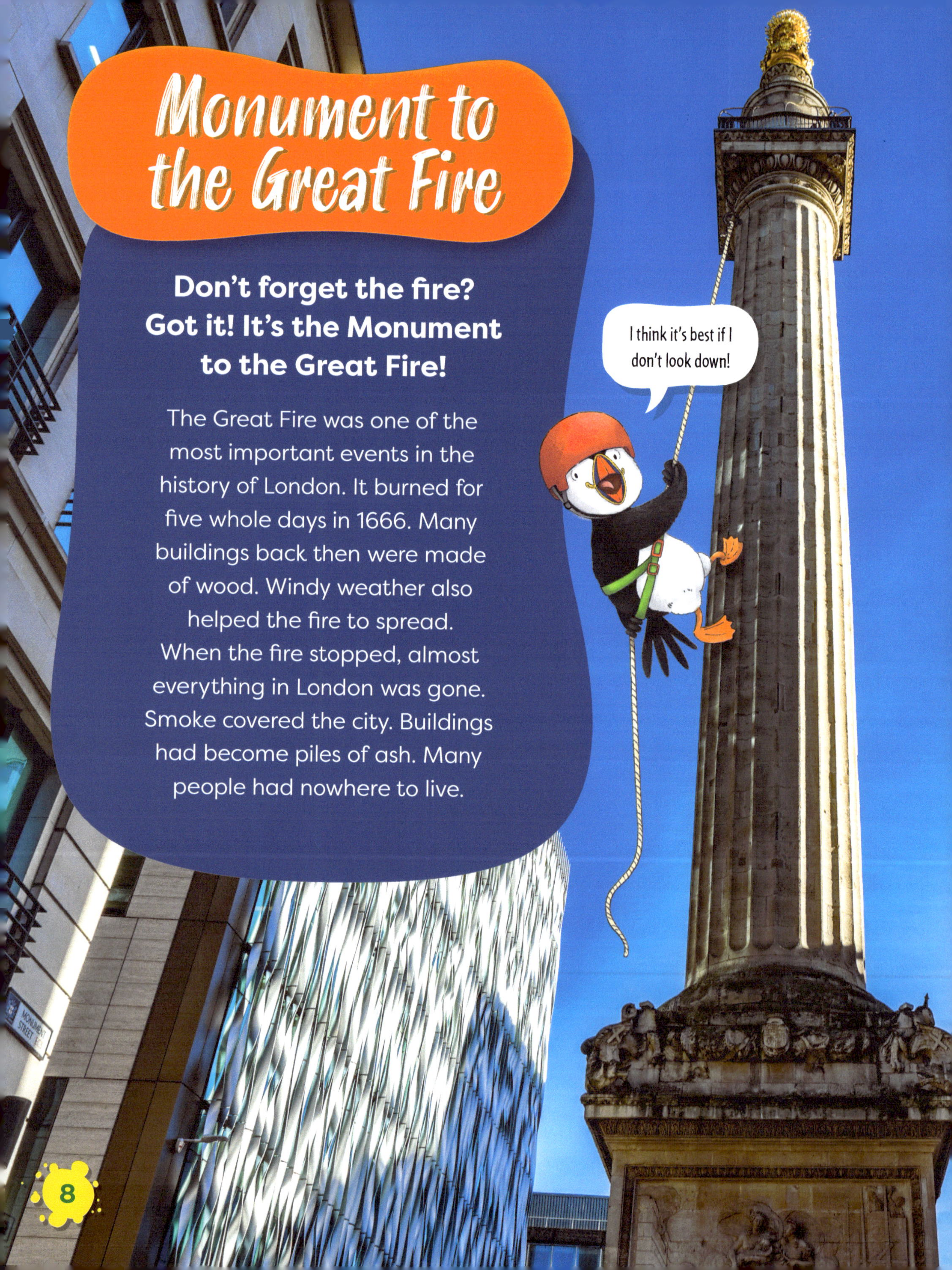

Monument to the Great Fire

Don't forget the fire? Got it! It's the Monument to the Great Fire!

The Great Fire was one of the most important events in the history of London. It burned for five whole days in 1666. Many buildings back then were made of wood. Windy weather also helped the fire to spread. When the fire stopped, almost everything in London was gone. Smoke covered the city. Buildings had become piles of ash. Many people had nowhere to live.

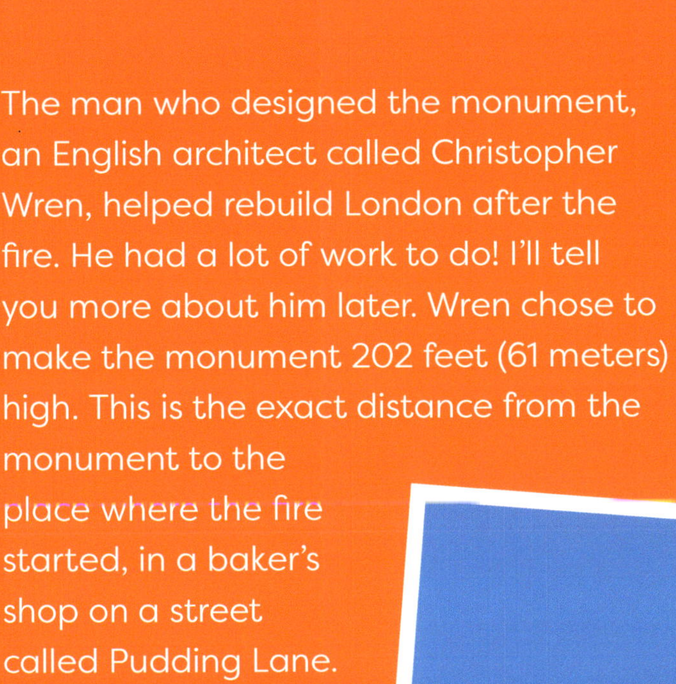

The man who designed the monument, an English architect called Christopher Wren, helped rebuild London after the fire. He had a lot of work to do! I'll tell you more about him later. Wren chose to make the monument 202 feet (61 meters) high. This is the exact distance from the monument to the place where the fire started, in a baker's shop on a street called Pudding Lane.

The bronze statue at the very top of the monument represents the flames of the fire.

If you're not scared of heights, you can look out over London from a viewing gallery that goes around the top of the monument. But be warned – you'll have to climb a narrow, winding staircase with over 300 stairs!

The mystery continues ... where will my next clue take me?

St Paul's Cathedral

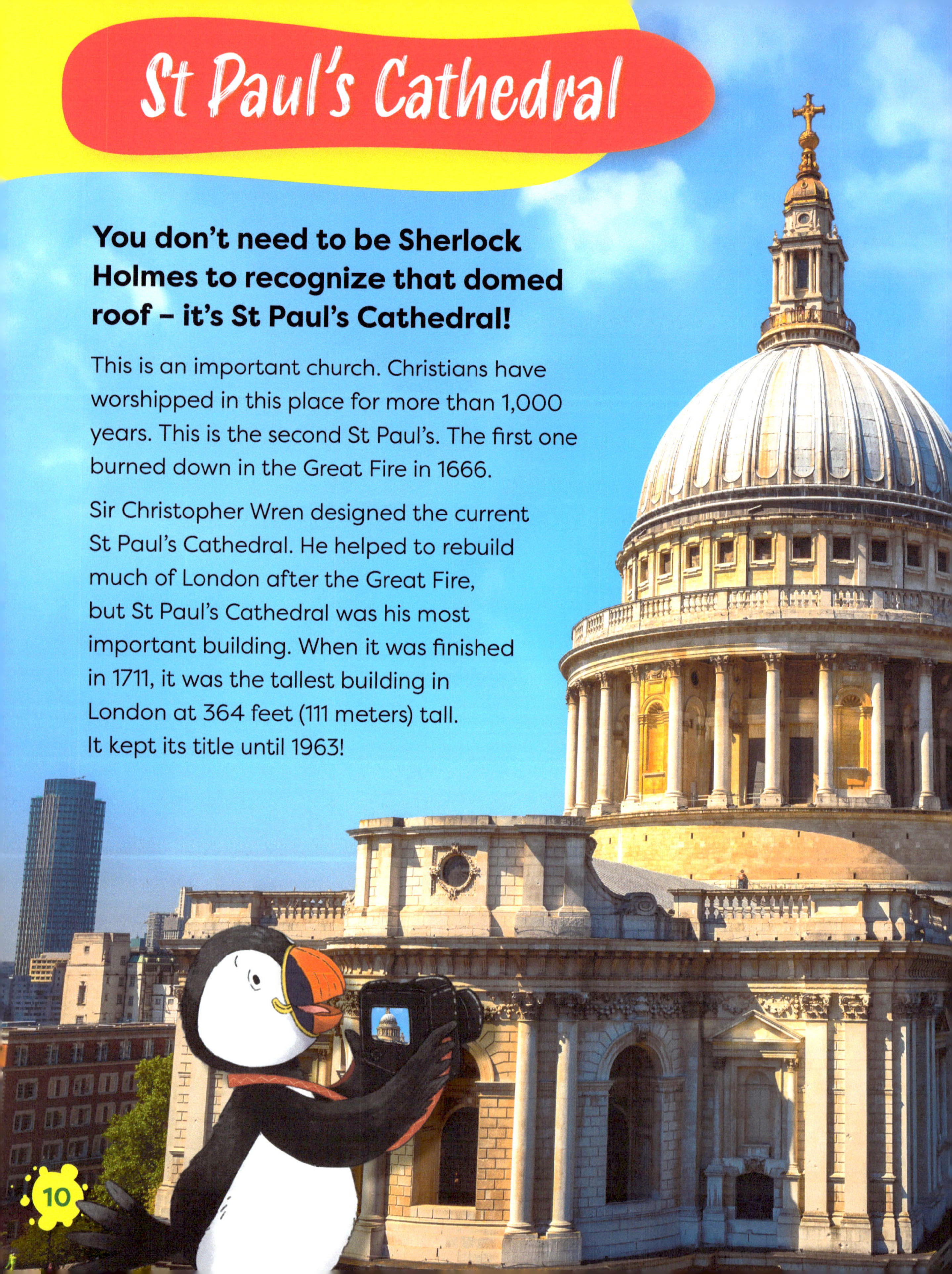

You don't need to be Sherlock Holmes to recognize that domed roof – it's St Paul's Cathedral!

This is an important church. Christians have worshipped in this place for more than 1,000 years. This is the second St Paul's. The first one burned down in the Great Fire in 1666.

Sir Christopher Wren designed the current St Paul's Cathedral. He helped to rebuild much of London after the Great Fire, but St Paul's Cathedral was his most important building. When it was finished in 1711, it was the tallest building in London at 364 feet (111 meters) tall. It kept its title until 1963!

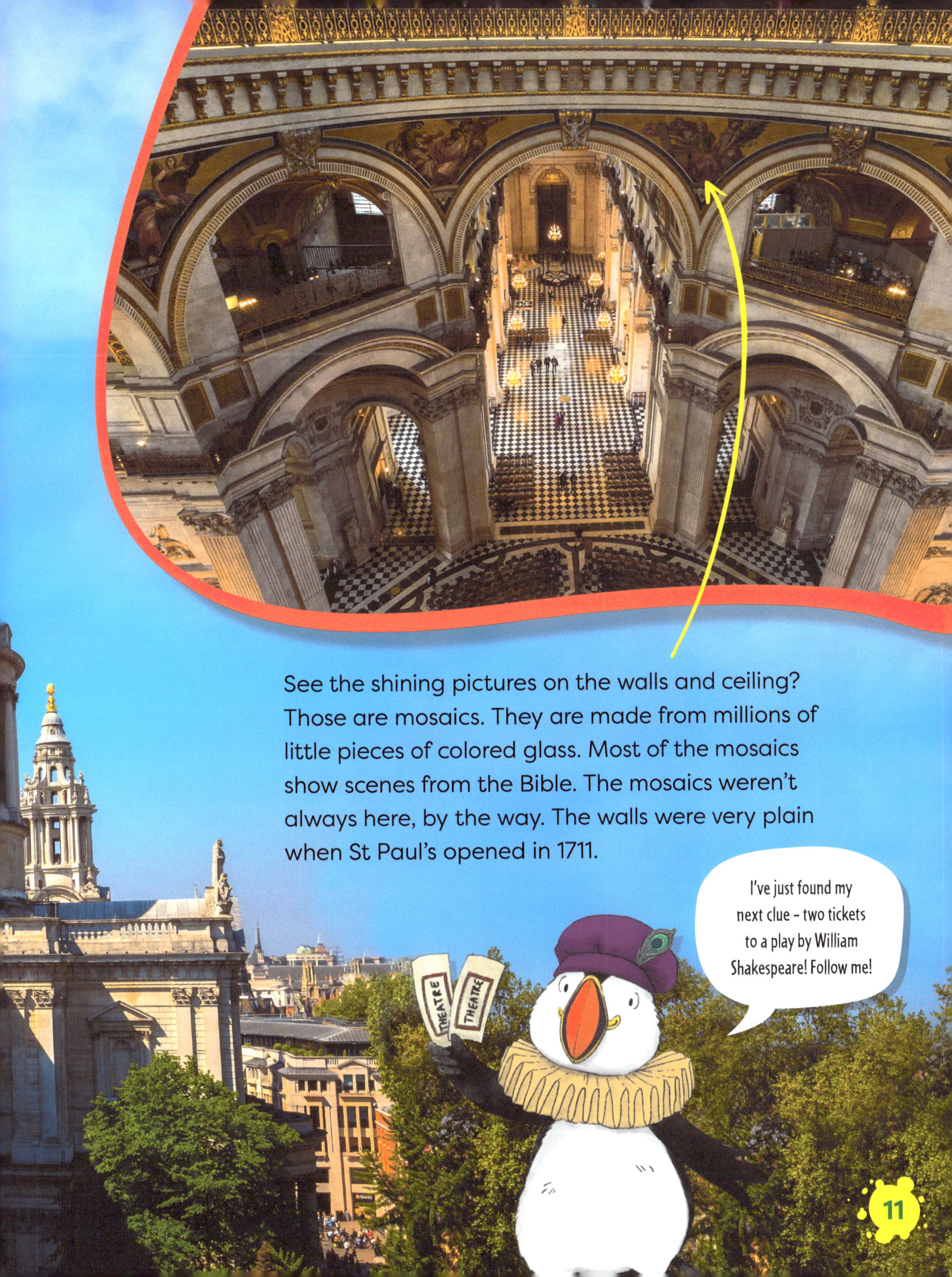

See the shining pictures on the walls and ceiling? Those are mosaics. They are made from millions of little pieces of colored glass. Most of the mosaics show scenes from the Bible. The mosaics weren't always here, by the way. The walls were very plain when St Paul's opened in 1711.

Shakespeare's Globe

No, we haven't traveled back in time! This is Shakespeare's Globe – a reconstruction of the theater where many of Shakespeare's plays were originally performed. You've heard of William Shakespeare, right? He may be the most famous playwright ever. You might have heard of some of the nearly 40 plays that he wrote, including *Romeo and Juliet*, *Macbeth* and *A Midsummer Night's Dream.*

The original Globe Theatre burned down in 1613. The second theater was torn down in 1644. This Globe opened in 1997. It's about a block away from where the other Globes were.

The actors at the Globe perform on a raised stage in the middle. Most of the audience stands around the stage, just like people did in the 1600's. Those people were called groundlings. Sitting down cost extra!

The Globe wasn't the only theater torn down in 1644. All theaters were outlawed by the government, because many people thought they were immoral (wicked). King Charles II brought theaters back again in the 1660's. The Drury Lane Theatre was the first, in 1663. It was built in the West End area. Today, the West End has theaters of all kinds.

The builders of the new theater tried to use the same materials as in the original Globe. They used brick, thatch, wooden pegs, and plaster. No metal screws or nails allowed!

The Shard

At 1,016 feet (310 meters) tall, the Shard isn't just the tallest building in London, or in the United Kingdom – it's the tallest building in Western Europe! Inside the skyscraper are offices, restaurants, hotels, and even apartments. There is also a viewing platform at the very top. On a clear day, you can see for 40 miles (64 kilometers)! The building opened to the public in 2012 and has been popular with tourists ever since.

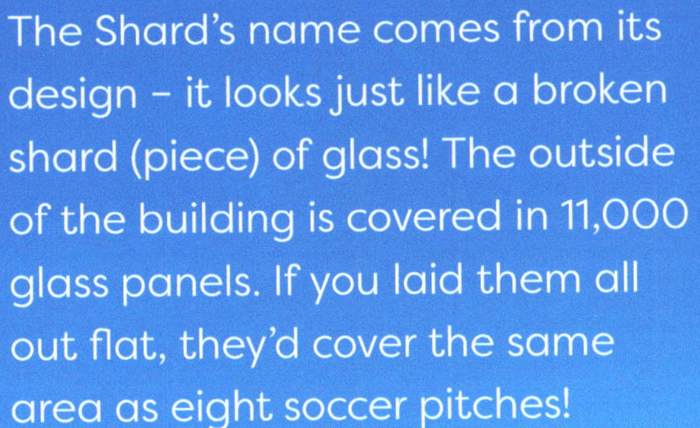

The Shard's name comes from its design – it looks just like a broken shard (piece) of glass! The outside of the building is covered in 11,000 glass panels. If you laid them all out flat, they'd cover the same area as eight soccer pitches!

Even the bathrooms in the Shard have amazing views! They are so high up that no one can see inside from the street below.

The Shard isn't the only skyscraper in London. There are many skyscrapers on the north side of the river. Some of the skyscrapers have very funny nicknames, such as the Gherkin and the Walkie-Talkie. Can you guess how they got their names?

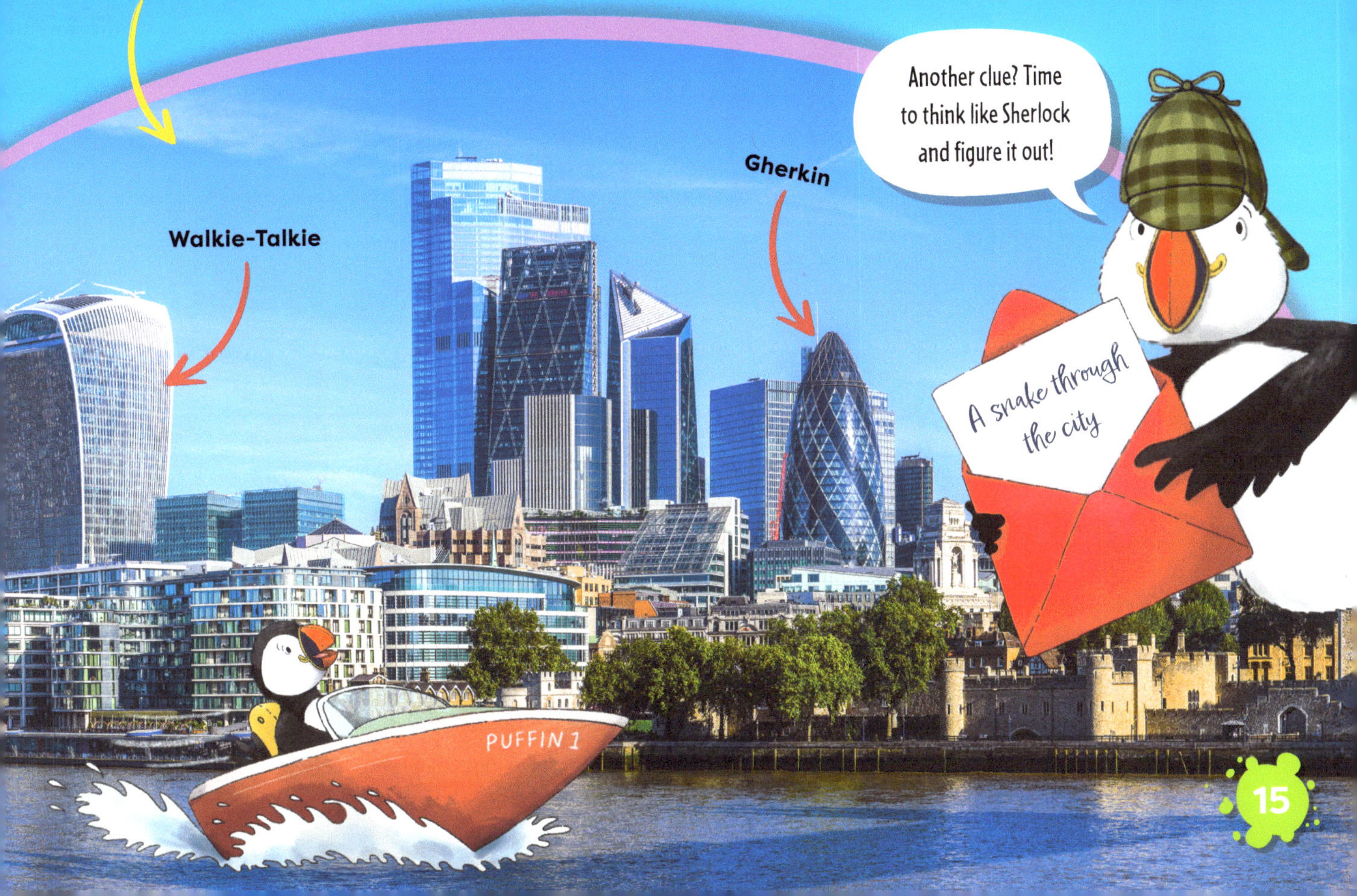

Another clue? Time to think like Sherlock and figure it out!

Gherkin

Walkie-Talkie

A snake through the city

PUFFIN 1

River Thames

I've got it! The River Thames is like a "snake" that twists and turns its way through the center of the city!

Bridges have crossed the Thames since Roman times. Do you know the name of the bridge over there? If you guessed London Bridge, guess again! This bridge is actually called Tower Bridge. It was built in the late 1800's.

The HMS *Belfast* is one of the few large ships in the Thames today. This warship was used in World War II. Today, it is a museum.

There aren't many ships on the River Thames today. In the 1800's and before, there were thousands of ships on the water. People used the river to bring goods in and out of the city every day. People from all over the world worked to load and unload the ships. Some of the biggest boat docks were not very far from Tower Bridge.

So what happened? Around the 1960's, ships became much bigger. They could not go as far up the river as smaller ships. Now ships dock in Tilbury, a town that's closer to the mouth of the river, at the North Sea.

Covent Garden

I've cracked the code! Outdoor fun and food in London has got to be Covent Garden!

In the past, this area was a massive outdoor market. And today there are still plenty of shops, places to eat, and fun things to watch.

Hundreds of years ago, many Londoners liked to shop in such outdoor markets as Covent Garden.

The market here sold mostly produce – that means fruits and vegetables – and flowers. (Before that, it was a huge garden for the cooks at Westminster Abbey.)

There are many things to do in the Covent Garden area. If you like listening to music, the Royal Opera House is nearby. So is the Drury Lane Theatre. But my favorite thing to do here is watch the buskers. Those are the people doing fun things out on the sidewalk. Buskers entertain people by playing music, juggling, dancing, or doing magic tricks. Have you ever seen a busker before?

British Museum

Visiting the British Museum in London is like traveling back in time and around the world.

It contains objects from many different cultures and civilizations. Some of its most famous exhibits include coffins and mummies from ancient Egypt, statues and carvings from ancient Greece, and Anglo-Saxon helmets and jewelry from England. Which exhibits would you like to see? I think I'll start with the ancient Egyptian collection.

The British Museum has been open to the public since 1759. The outside of the building looks very traditional because it was built in the 1800's. However, the center of the museum is very modern. This new space opened to the public in 2000.

The British Museum is just one of London's many museums. Other popular museums here include the Natural History Museum, where you can learn about plants, animals, and planet Earth, the Science Museum, and the Victoria and Albert Museum, which focuses on art and design. The best thing about the museums in London is that most of them are totally free to visit!

London Eye

It's hard to miss the London Eye! You can see this giant Ferris wheel from across the city.

A Ferris wheel is a ride that you usually find at a fair or amusement park. Perhaps you've been on one? The London Eye stands right next to the River Thames, across the river from Parliament and Big Ben. At 443 feet (135 meters) tall, it was the tallest Ferris wheel in the world until 2006.

The London Eye opened in 2000. It was only supposed to stay open for five years, but it was so popular that they decided to keep it up permanently. Today it is one of the most popular tourist destinations in the United Kingdom.

Visitors ride in the 32 pods around the outside of the wheel. There's space for 25 people in each pod. The wheel moves so slowly that it doesn't usually stop for passengers to get on or off. It takes about 30 minutes to go all the way around.

Parliament

I recognize those windows! They come from the long building next to Big Ben.

Its official name is the Palace of Westminster, but these days, most people call it Parliament for short. It looks fancy, right? Most of these buildings were built after a great fire in 1834. But a palace and other government buildings have stood here for 1,000 years!

Millions of people live in England, Scotland, Wales, and Northern Ireland. These are the parts that make up the United Kingdom. Voters all across the United Kingdom elect men and women to speak for them in the House of Commons. That is the most important group in Parliament. Anyone can watch the members of Parliament talk back and forth from the public galleries. (That's where visitors sit.)

There's an excellent view of Parliament from the River Thames!

The other group is the House of Lords. They are not elected by voters. The chamber (room) where they hold debates is decorated in red.

The monarch of the United Kingdom gives a speech in the House of Lords every year at a ceremony called the State Opening of Parliament.

The prime minister is the leader of the government. The prime minister lives at 10 Downing Street, which is nicknamed "Number 10."

That's a real brainteaser! But I think I know the answer – follow me!

Big Ben

That was a tricky riddle to solve!

Only a true Londoner would know that Big Ben is technically the nickname of the bell inside the clock tower, and not the name of the clock! However, most people use the name Big Ben to refer to all three things – the clock, the clock tower and the bell! The tower's official name is Elizabeth Tower. It was named after Elizabeth II, who was queen of the United Kingdom of Great Britain and Northern Ireland.

Big Ben is the Parliament clock tower. It's probably the most famous clock in the world! There is a clock face on each of the tower's four sides, so people can see the time wherever they are!

Everything about Big Ben is massive. The Big Ben bell weighs 15,100 tons (13,700 tonnes), which is as much as two male African elephants! Elizabeth Tower is the height of 21 London buses on top of each other. The minute hands on the clocks are almost as tall as a giraffe!

Wedding bells and famous graves

I know exactly where Lord Percival Pigeon's next clue is ... just around the corner!

Westminster Abbey

Welcome to Westminster Abbey!

This is a special Christian church. Different parts of the building were made at different times. King Edward the Confessor started the job in 1065. Most of what you see now, though, was built later by King Henry III in the 1200's. Guess where he lived? Just around the corner, in the Palace of Westminster. He built the first palace at Westminster so he could live close to the abbey and watch over its construction.

Many churches have places to bury dead people outside in the churchyard. At Westminster Abbey, people are buried inside. Most of the people who get a spot are very famous. They include kings and queens, prime ministers, scientists, poets, and authors.

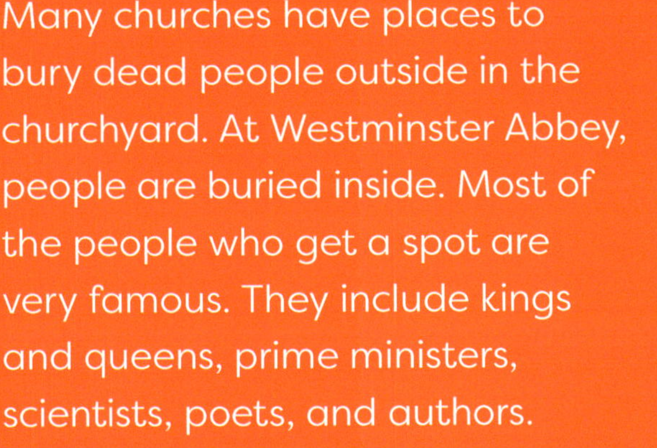

One famous person buried in Westminster Abbey is Queen Elizabeth I. She died in 1603. This is her tomb.

Westminster Abbey is built in the Gothic style, like many churches in Europe. Gothic buildings have high, decorated ceilings and big colored glass windows. These windows are known as stained glass windows. Aren't they beautiful?

Who is this? And more importantly, where can I find him?!

Trafalgar Square

Found it! This statue is on a very tall pillar in Trafalgar Square.

The statue and pillar are known as Nelson's Column. The man at the top is Horatio Nelson, who won many sea battles in the 1800's. There are other statues here as well, including four lions at the bottom of Nelson's Column.

People come to Trafalgar Square to sit and rest, have a drink at a café, and watch the world go by! There is also a big celebration here on December 31st to celebrate New Year's Eve. Maybe I'll have to come back for another visit!

The lions at the base of Nelson's Column are said to protect it!

The center of London has many open spaces. Squares, like Trafalgar Square here, are open spaces with a square shape. Circuses are open spaces that are shaped like circles. The most famous circus in London is Piccadilly Circus. It has lots of large video advertisements.

Buckingham Palace

**Furry hats flying a flag?
That's got to be Buckingham Palace!**

This is where some members of the royal family live today. In the past, kings and queens lived in the Palace of Westminster, which is where Parliament is now.

Buckingham Palace has an incredible 775 rooms. This includes 240 bedrooms, 92 offices, 19 state rooms (which are used for formal events), and 78 bathrooms! The royal family holds many special events and parties at Buckingham Palace. Over 50,000 people attend these events every year, so all those rooms must come in handy!

The furry hats and red coats are part of the King's Guard uniform. Their hats are called bearskins. The King's Guard are soldiers in the British Army.

And here's the flag! It's called a Union Jack. Did you know that this flag acts as a code? It tells me that the monarch is not home today. (Monarch is a big word for king or queen.) If the monarch were home, we would see a different flag, called the Royal Standard.
The King's Guard are very serious. They won't smile at us, even if we make funny faces. It must be hard for them not to laugh!
Another mystery to solve – I think I'm going to need my wallet for this one!
Harrods

Harrods

This is Harrods, a very famous department store. It's found in a neighborhood called Knightsbridge.

All of the shops along this road seem very posh (that's a word that means fancy), but Harrods is the fanciest of them all! The founder, Henry Charles Harrod, started the business as a grocery store in 1849. It has come a long way since then!

Harrods sells all sorts of things. I've heard there are more than 300 departments! You can buy clothes, electronics, toys, gifts, and even furniture! It also has over 20 restaurants and cafés where you can eat and rest after a long day of shopping. Shopping or food ... I don't know what to do first!

Harrods is famous for its afternoon tea. You can order cakes, little sandwiches, and scones, which are sweet biscuits served with thick cream and jam. And to drink? Tea of course! This light meal has been a special time in the day in England for almost 200 years.

Hyde Park

Believe it or not, there are quite a few green, grassy places in London! Hyde Park is one of my favorites.

It's located behind Buckingham Palace and has been owned by the royal family since 1536. It has been used for many different things over the years. King Henry VIII used it for hunting. In 1665, Londoners camped here to avoid getting sick from the plague.

The Great Exhibition of 1851, the first World's Fair, was in Hyde Park. An exhibition is a big show of things. It lasted for months, and millions of people visited from around the world. It was an exciting time in science and industry. The fair taught visitors about machinery and other inventions.

More recently, some parts of the 2012 Summer Olympics happened in the park. Swimmers used the Serpentine, a lake in the middle of the park.

Speakers' Corner is found in the northeast corner of Hyde Park. People go there to debate and argue. They stand up on boxes and stools and shout about politics and other topics.

At the southeast corner of the park is Wellington Arch. The statue on top represents Nike, the Greek goddess of victory. She's riding a chariot pulled by four horses.

London Underground

A circle with a horizontal line through it is the symbol of the London Underground.

This massive network of underground trains is the fastest way to get around the city. Londoners call it the Tube. The Oyster card is the payment card needed to travel.

Some of the tracks in the London Underground are more than 150 years old. In the 1800's, workers dug long tunnels under the ground. London was the first city in the whole world to have underground trains. (Many cities have them now.) Today, more than 250 miles

(400 kilometers) of rail lines snake beneath London's streets, connecting 272 different stations. Over 1.3 billion passengers ride on the Tube every year. During World War II, many Londoners camped in the Underground stations at night for safety. They slept on the floors, the escalators, and even the tracks. It was crowded! But it helped protect them from enemy bombs.

This is the London Underground map. The different colors represent different underground lines. If you want to change lines, you need to go to a station where the lines cross over! The boat symbols show places where you can catch a boat to take you up or down the River Thames.

London Zoo

There's only one place in London where you can spot tigers (I hope)!

London Zoo has been here since 1828, making it one of the world's oldest zoos. It is home to animals from every continent on Earth, all in one place! Almost 700 kinds of animals live here – from corals and sea jellies to lemurs and butterflies. But no puffins!

If you're feeling brave, you can see spiders, crocodiles, and king cobras. Or if you want something less scary, why not visit London Zoo's pygmy hippos. They're much smaller than regular hippos and very cute!

The penguin pool at London Zoo has a glass wall so that you can see how the penguins swim and dive underwater.

As well as being a fun day out, the zoo also helps to protect animals. It keeps endangered animals safe, and zookeepers help them to have babies. Their babies are later released back into the wild. Scientists also study the animals at London Zoo to learn more about how they live and behave.

London Zoo is at the north end of Regent's Park. Hundreds and hundreds of years ago, the park was a royal hunting ground. Today, it's a popular spot for picnics, walks and games.

Baker Street

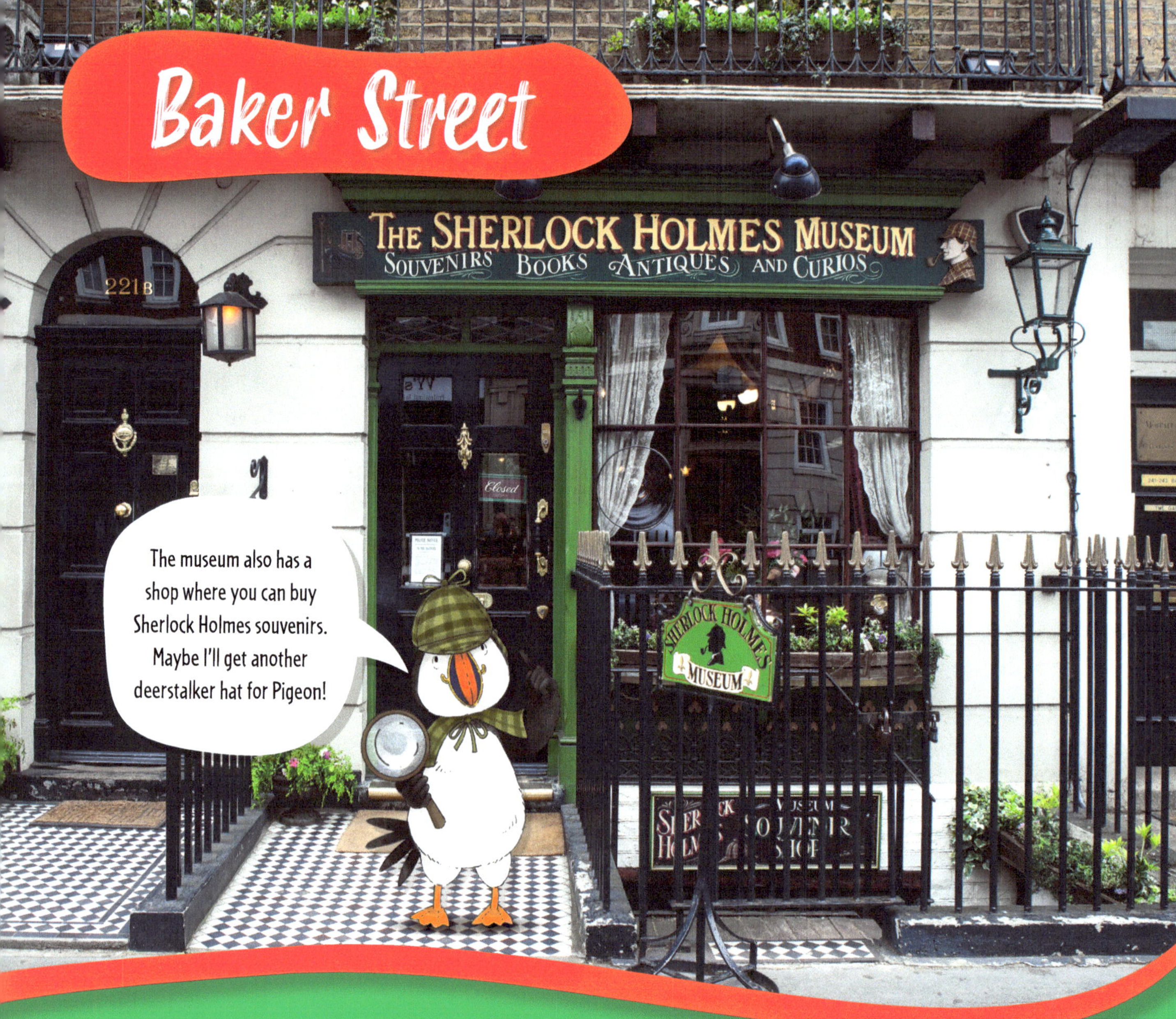

Home sweet Holmes!

In the Sherlock Holmes books, the detective lives at 221B Baker Street, London. Sherlock Holmes wasn't real, of course, but Baker Street is! Today there are several attractions around Baker Street for fans of the famous detective.

The Sherlock Holmes Museum is found in a house from the same time period as Sherlock Holmes. The rooms of the house have been decorated with furniture and objects from that time. Visiting the museum is like visiting Sherlock Holmes's very own apartment! There are also replicas of objects from Holmes's most famous cases.

The tiles at the Baker Street Underground station are decorated to look like Sherlock Holmes. This isn't the only London Underground station with special tiles. The South Kensington Underground station has tiles decorated with animals to represent the nearby Natural History Museum!

LONDON MAP

London Zoo
British Museum
The Sherlock Holmes Museum
Baker Street
Regent's Park
Trafalgar Square
Hyde Park
Harrods
Buckingham Palace
Westminster Abbey

St Paul's Cathedral
Monument to the Great Fire
Covent Garden
Shakespeare's Globe
Parliament
Big Ben
Tower of London
London Eye
The Shard
River Thames

A Day in London

Black pudding is a type of blood sausage made from pork or beef.

Begin your morning with a full English breakfast! This commonly includes tea, eggs, bacon, tomatoes, mushrooms, and baked beans. Don't forget the black pudding!

Piccadilly Circus

Hop on a double-decker bus and tour the city. Make sure to check out Windsor Castle, Kew Gardens, and Piccadilly Circus.

Make a quick stop for some delicious fish and chips before heading to Wembley Stadium. Picture yourself cheering for the England National Football Team as they kick the ball up and down the pitch.

Wembley is the second largest stadium in all of Europe and has 90,000 seats!

Squeeze in some time for a cup of afternoon tea and treats at world-famous Harrods.

Round out your busy day in London with an evening show at the Royal Opera House. Whether you see a ballet or an opera, you are sure to remember this world-class artistic experience.

Where Am I?

Destination 1

This is a long building on the River Thames next to Big Ben.

The House of Commons and the House of Lords meet and work here.

Anyone can watch U.K. government officials from the public galleries.

Destination 2

This building flies the Union Jack or Royal Standard flags as a code.

The guards wear red coats and furry hats called bearskins.

The royal family lives in this massive palace with 775 rooms!

Destination 3

Here you can find offices, restaurants, hotels, and apartments all in one place!

This is one of the many newer skyscrapers found on the north side of the River Thames.

On clear days, you can see for 40 miles from the top of this tallest building in Western Europe.

Destination 4

People often come here to relax, enjoy the atmosphere, and spend time outside in the busy city.

Every December, thousands of people gather here to ring in the new year!

This destination can be recognized by Nelson's Column and the surrounding statues of four large lions.

Destination 5

This attraction was meant to be open for only five years, but because it was so popular, it is now a permanent fixture on the River Thames.

Catch amazing 360° views of London from this 443-foot-tall ride.

A full rotation on this massive Ferris wheel takes about 30 minutes!

Destination 6

In the past, Londoners shopped in outdoor markets like this one.

Today, people come here to purchase produce, fresh flowers, and other goods.

People also watch buskers juggle, play music, dance, or even do magic tricks on the sidewalk!

Answers on page 55

Photos from London

Westminster Abbey

British Museum

Harrods

Shakespeare's Globe
YOUNG HEARTS
23 APRIL - 10 OCTOBER
Big Ben
TELEPHONE

St Paul's Cathedral

Tower of London

Engage Your Reader

Activate background knowledge, set the purpose for reading, and monitor comprehension with this tried-and-true reading strategy!

Work with your reader(s) to create a KWL chart. Take some time to discuss what students already KNOW about London as well as what they WONDER about the city. You will revisit what they LEARNED after reading the book.

KNOW	WONDER	LEARNED

1. Have readers preview the structure of this text by flipping through the pages. Page 5 describes how clues are included for Norrie the puffin's next destinations.
2. Set the tone for reading: *As you read, think about all the different places in London and how history, culture, and people have shaped them into what they are today.*
3. After reading each section, revisit the KWL chart. Brainstorm what readers LEARNED from this section and add it to the chart. Your reader can add other wonderings they may have had, too!

Consider these questions to guide the brainstorming process:

- Why is location important to places, history, and culture?
- What patterns do you notice in the placement of things around the city of London?
- What makes London unique?

Use these comprehension questions to help your reader(s) check their understanding as they navigate the text.

p. 6-7 What are beefeaters? What jobs have they historically performed, and what jobs do they perform now?

Why do the ravens guarding the Tower of London have clipped wings?

p. 8-9 What happened during the Great Fire of 1666?

How does the material used in the monument represent the fire?

p. 10-11 Why do you believe mosaics were not added to St Paul's Cathedral until 1711?

Who was Sir Christopher Wren, and why is he important to London's history?

p. 12-13 Why might the builders not have used metal screws or nails when constructing the New Globe Theatre?

p. 14-15 Although London is a very old city with plenty of historic architecture, it also includes many modern buildings. Why do you think many newer skyscrapers are all built in the same general area on the north side of the River Thames?

p. 16-17 Why is the River Thames less busy today than it was in the 1800's?

p. 18-19 How has Covent Garden changed and developed over time?

What would you enjoy doing most at Covent Garden? Why?

p. 20-21 What types of art can you find at the British Museum?

p. 22-23 The London Eye was intended to be open for only five years but is now a permanent part of the city. Why do you think this attraction is so popular?

If you visited London, would you ride the London Eye? Why or why not?

p. 24-25 How does the organization of Parliament with the House of Commons and the House of Lords compare to the organization of your government?

p. 26-27 List and describe Big Ben's three major components.

What fact about Big Ben stood out to you the most? Why?

p. 28-29 What is Westminster Abbey, and why is it famous?

p. 30-31 What would you do if you visited Trafalgar Square or Piccadilly Circus in London?

p. 32-33 Explain how the flag above Buckingham Palace is actually a code.

What do you find most impressive about Buckingham Palace?

p. 34-35 What is Harrods, and why is it so famous?

p. 36-37 How has Hyde Park been used and changed over time?

What would you enjoy doing at Hyde Park in London?

p. 38-39 What is the London Underground, and why is it an important part of the city?

p. 40-41 How does the London Zoo help support endangered animals?

p. 42-43 What is Baker Street, and why is it so famous in London?

Extend Through Writing

Norrie the puffin just took you on a tour of London, England, in the United Kingdom! Based on the places highlighted in this book, where would you like to visit in London?

Your written response should include:

- An introduction, including a general statement about London
- At least three places you would like to visit and at least three reasons why these places interest you
- A conclusion in which you briefly restate your interest in these three famous London destinations

Copy this graphic organizer onto another sheet of paper or visit **www.worldbook.com/resources** to download and print a copy. Use it to help you plan your writing.

Introduction:		
Destination 1	Destination 2	Destination 3
Reason 1	Reason 1	Reason 1
Reason 2	Reason 2	Reason 2
Reason 3	Reason 3	Reason 3
Conclusion:		

Answers

Where Am I? answers, p. 48-49:

1. Parliament, 2. Buckingham Palace, 3. The Shard, 4. Trafalgar Square, 5. London Eye, 6. Covent Garden

Comprehension question answers, p. 53:

p. 6-7

Beefeaters work at the Tower of London. In the past they guarded the tower, but now they give tours and greet visitors.

p. 8-9

The Great Fire of 1666 burned for five days and destroyed the majority of the city. The bronze statue of the top of the monument was built to look like the fire's flames.

p. 10-11

Answers may vary.

Sir Christopher Wren designed the current St Paul's Cathedral, which was the tallest building in London for over 250 years!

p. 12-13

The builders of the new Globe wanted the theater to feel authentic to the original, so they used such crude materials as wooden pegs and thatch.

p. 14-15

Answers may vary but will likely include inferences about new construction in underdeveloped areas of the city as opposed to historic ones.

p. 16-17

The River Thames is not as busy today as it once was because today's ships are too large for the river itself.

p. 18-19

Today, Covent Garden is an outdoor hub in London, just as it was in the past. Whereas people once shopped mainly for produce and flowers, today's visitors purchase additional products and watch public entertainment.

Answers may vary.

p. 20-21

The British Museum is world famous! Visitors can find all sorts of art, including coffins and mummies from ancient Egypt, statues and carvings from ancient Greece, Anglo-Saxon helmets, jewelry from England, and more!

p. 22-23

Answers may vary.

p. 24-25

Answers may vary. For example, readers may compare the structure of Parliament to that of the United States Congress.

p. 26-27

When most people think of Big Ben, they picture the clock, clock tower, and the bell of Elizabeth Tower. But Big Ben actually refers to only the bell itself! Answers related to reasoning may vary.

p. 28-29

Westminster Abbey is a special Christian church that houses the graves of famous kings and queens, prime ministers, scientists, poets, and authors.

p. 30-31

Answers may vary.

p. 32-33

Buckingham Palace flies a flag that acts as a code. The palace flies the Royal Standard flag when the monarch is home, but it flies the Union Jack flag when the monarch is away.

p. 34-35

Harrods is a famous department store that opened in 1849! In addition to great shopping, Londoners and tourists alike enjoy its afternoon tea and snacks.

p. 36-37

Hyde Park has been used for many purposes since 1536. The royal family used it for hunting, it housed people avoiding the plague in 1665, and it was the location of the first World's Fair in 1857. More recently, it hosted some Summer Olympics events in 2012. Today, regular Londoners enjoy visiting the park to spend time outdoors.

Answers may vary.

p. 38-39

The London Underground is a massive system of trains that connect the entire city! People use them to travel around safely and efficiently.

p. 40-41

London Zoo supports endangered animals by keeping them safe. They also breed animal babies that are eventually released back to the wild to be studied.

p. 42-43

Baker Street is the home of the fictional character Sherlock Holmes, but in real life it is a museum and gift shop! Baker Street is a famous London destination because of the classic detective stories.

Glossary

bearskin *(BAIR SKIHN)* A tall, black fur cap worn by some soldiers in the British Army. The bearskin is part of the dress uniform of the household troops of the British sovereign.

beefeater *(BEEF EE tuhr)* A warder, or special guard, of the Tower of London

groundling *(GROWND lihng)* A member of a theater audience who traditionally stood in the pit below the stage

Londoner *(LUHN duhn er)* A person who lives in the city of London

monarch *(MON uhrk)* A king, queen, emperor, empress, or other ruler

palace *(PAL ihs)* A large, fancy building, usually the place where a king or queen lives

plague *(playg)* A bad disease caused by living things called bacteria. Fleas with bubonic plague give it to people by biting them.

Tube *(toob)* Another name for the London subway system. Its official name is the London Underground.

Index

www.ingramcontent.com/pod-product-compliance
Ingram Content Group UK Ltd.
Pitfield, Milton Keynes, MK11 3LW, UK
UKHW060105300726
14090UKWH00003B/377

* 9 7 8 0 7 1 6 6 5 3 2 8 8 *